INSPIRATIONAL
Picture Quotes
About
LEARNING
GABI RUPP
lean jumpstart

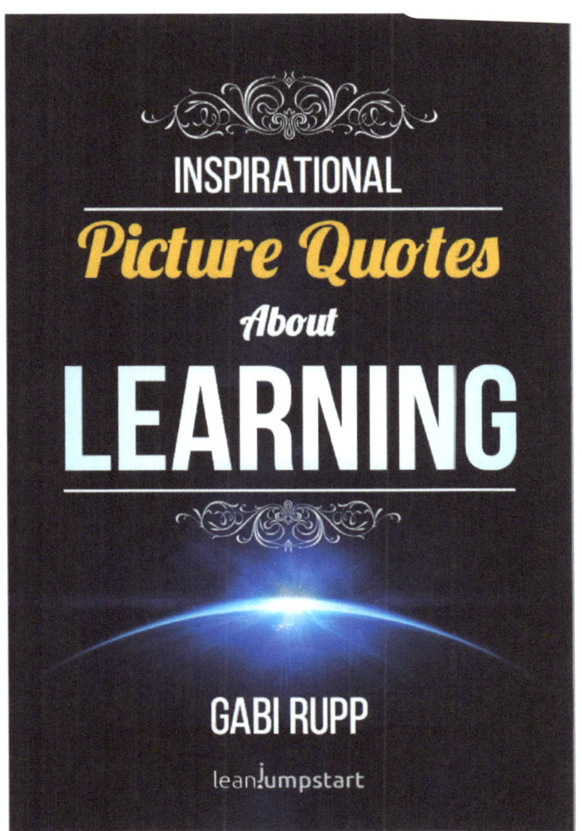

To: ....

From: ....

Dear reader,
this is a book to always carry with you
and cherish, to be there whenever you need
to be inspired. These unique learning quotes and
sayings will encourage you to keep learning and
expanding your education. They remind us that
learning is the key to life, unlocking otherwise
hidden joys and satisfactions.

Thank you and remember lifelong learning is
like a fitness club for your brain.

Gabi Rupp

STAY
HUNGRY,
STAY
FOOLISH.
STEVE JOBS

Inspiration

We learn more
by looking for
the answer to
a question and
not finding it
than we do
from learning
the answer itself.
~Lloyd Alexander

A sense of
curiosity is
nature's
original
school of
education.
~Smiley Blanton

He who is
afraid to ask
is ashamed
of learning.
~Danish
Proverb

I respect
faith,
but doubt is
what gets you
an education.
~Wilson Mizner

Curiosity

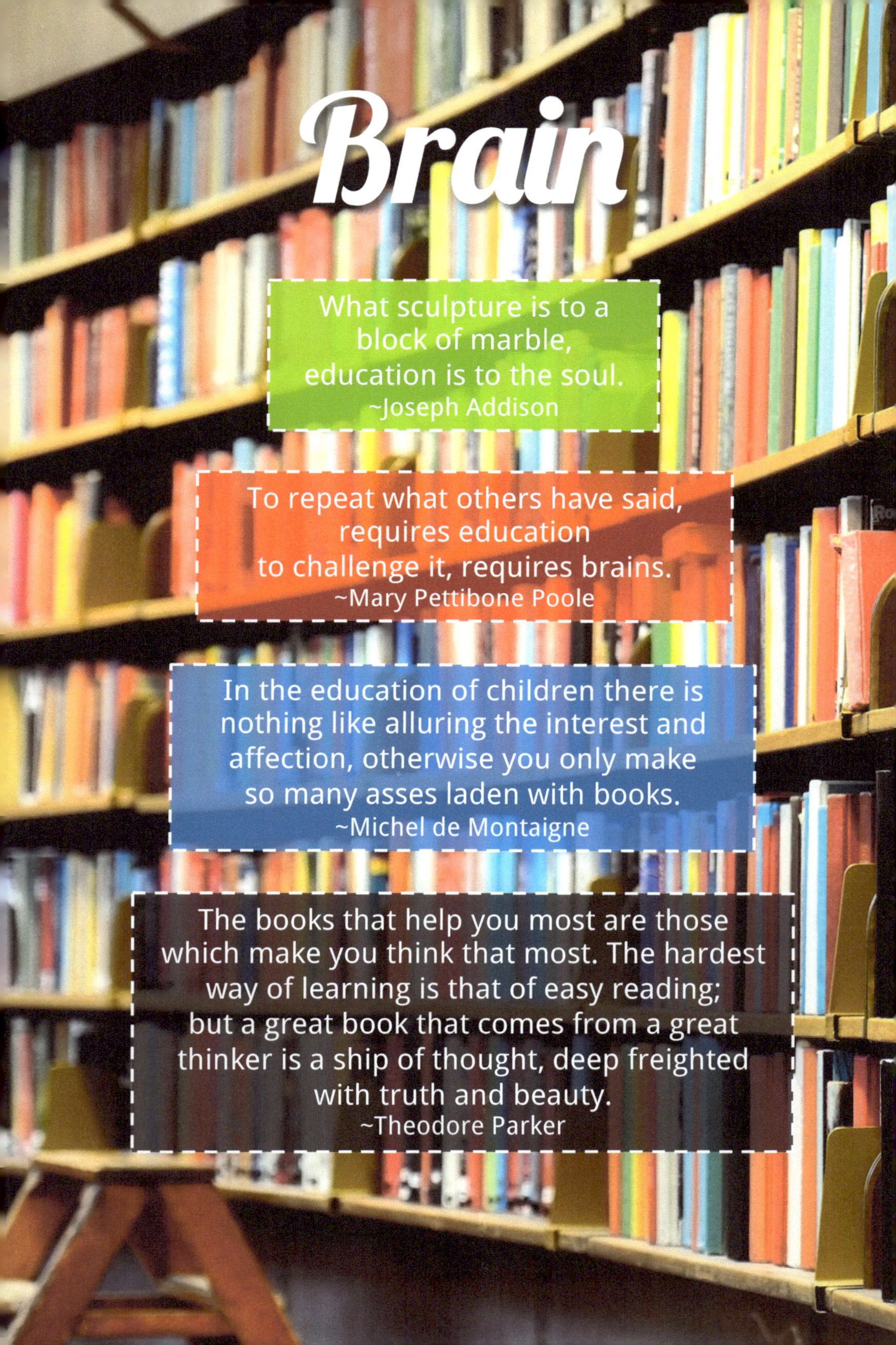

Brain

What sculpture is to a
block of marble,
education is to the soul.
~Joseph Addison

To repeat what others have said,
requires education
to challenge it, requires brains.
~Mary Pettibone Poole

In the education of children there is
nothing like alluring the interest and
affection, otherwise you only make
so many asses laden with books.
~Michel de Montaigne

The books that help you most are those
which make you think that most. The hardest
way of learning is that of easy reading;
but a great book that comes from a great
thinker is a ship of thought, deep freighted
with truth and beauty.
~Theodore Parker

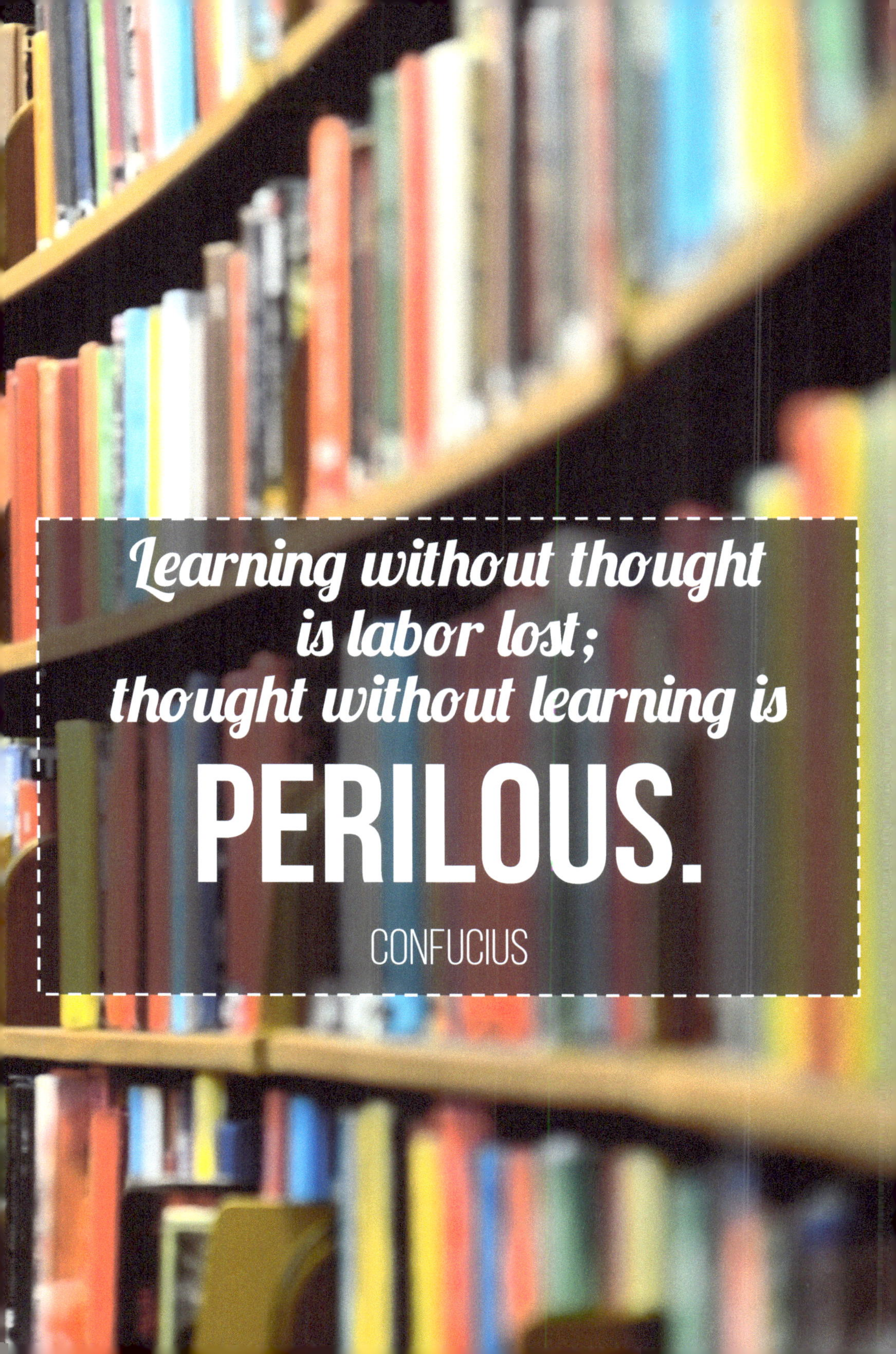

Learning without thought
is labor lost;
thought without learning is
PERILOUS.
CONFUCIUS

Play is often talked about as if it were a relief from serious learning. But for children play is serious learning.
~Fred Rogers
The most effective kind of education is that a child should play amongst lovely things.
~Plato

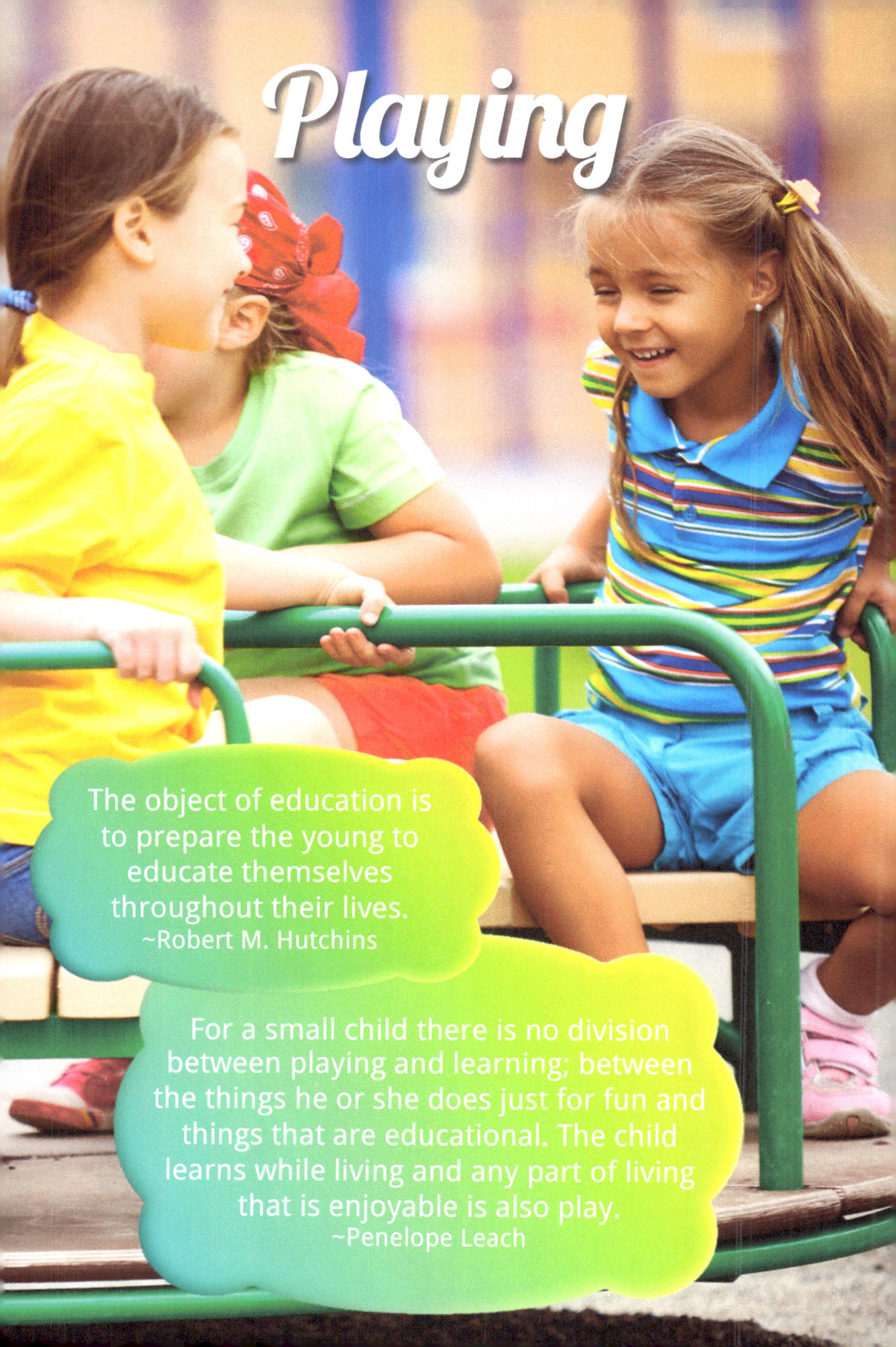

Playing

The object of education is
to prepare the young to
educate themselves
throughout their lives.
~Robert M. Hutchins

For a small child there is no division
between playing and learning; between
the things he or she does just for fun and
things that are educational. The child
learns while living and any part of living
that is enjoyable is also play.
~Penelope Leach

Liberty

The library is the temple of learning,
and learning has liberated more people
than all the wars in history.
~Carl T. Rowan

Education is a better
safeguard of liberty
than a standing army.
~Edward Everett

Liberty without learning
is always in peril;
learning without liberty
is always in vain.
~John F. Kennedy

Education is
too important
to be left solely
to the educators.
~Francis Keppel

Positive
reinforcement
is a powerful
teaching tool.
~Heidi McDonald

The things taught in
colleges and schools
are not an education,
but the means of
education.
~Ralph Waldo
Emerson

A child
only educated
at school is an
uneducated
child.
~George
Santayana

School

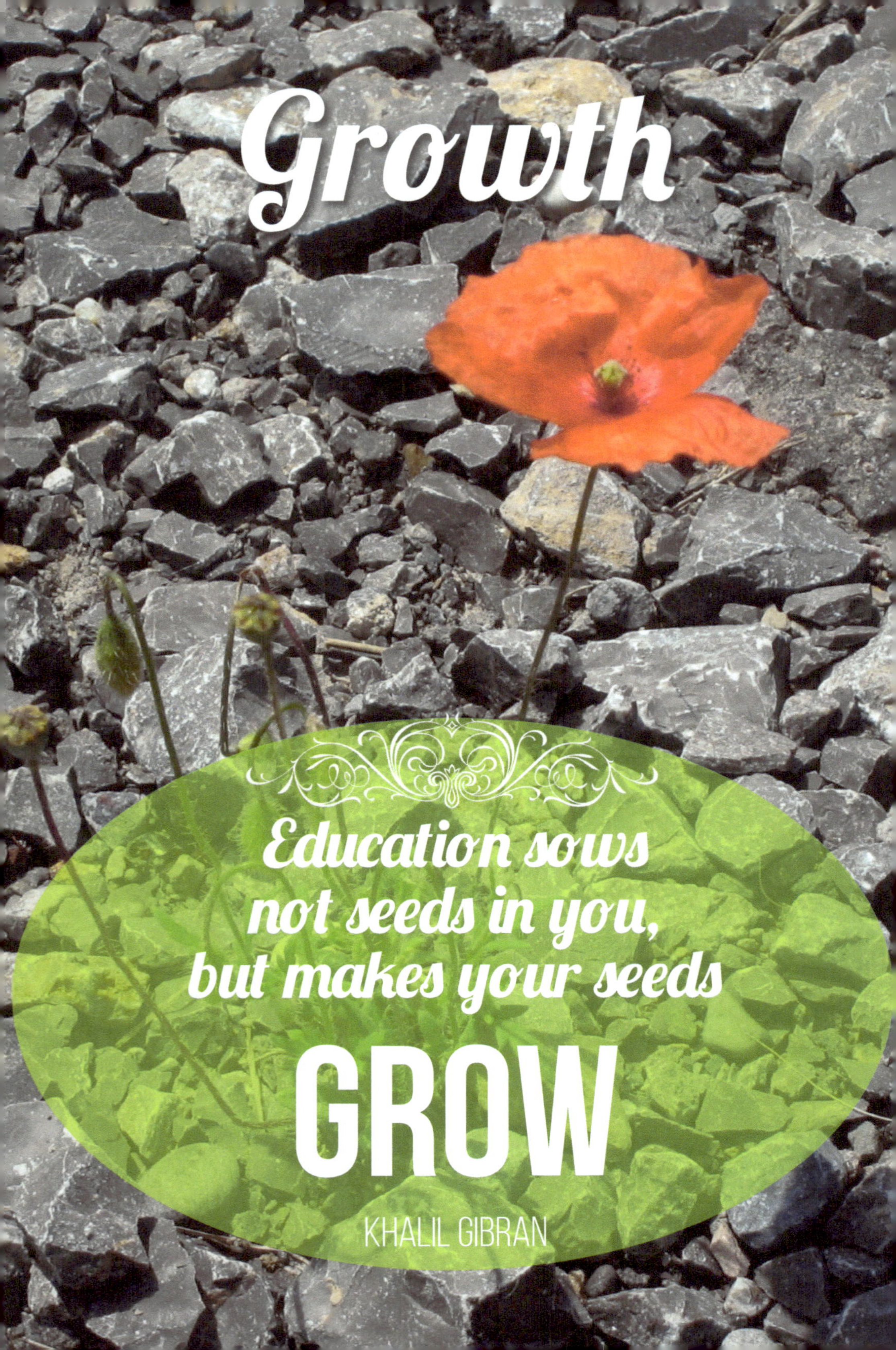

Growth
Education sows
not seeds in you,
but makes your seeds
GROW
KHALIL GIBRAN

I'm constantly learning,
and that is the greatest gift
of life in my opinion –
to always be learning
and growing.
~Kristin Chenoweth

The purpose of learning
is growth, and our minds,
unlike our bodies, can
continue growing as we
continue to live.
~Morris Adler

If you consider
what are called the virtues in
mankind, you will find their
growth is assisted
by education and cultivation.
~Xenophon

In terms of doing work and in terms
of learning and evolving as a person,
you just grow more when you get
more people's perspectives... I really
try and live the mission of the
company and... keep everything else
in my life extremely simple.
~Mark Zuckerberg

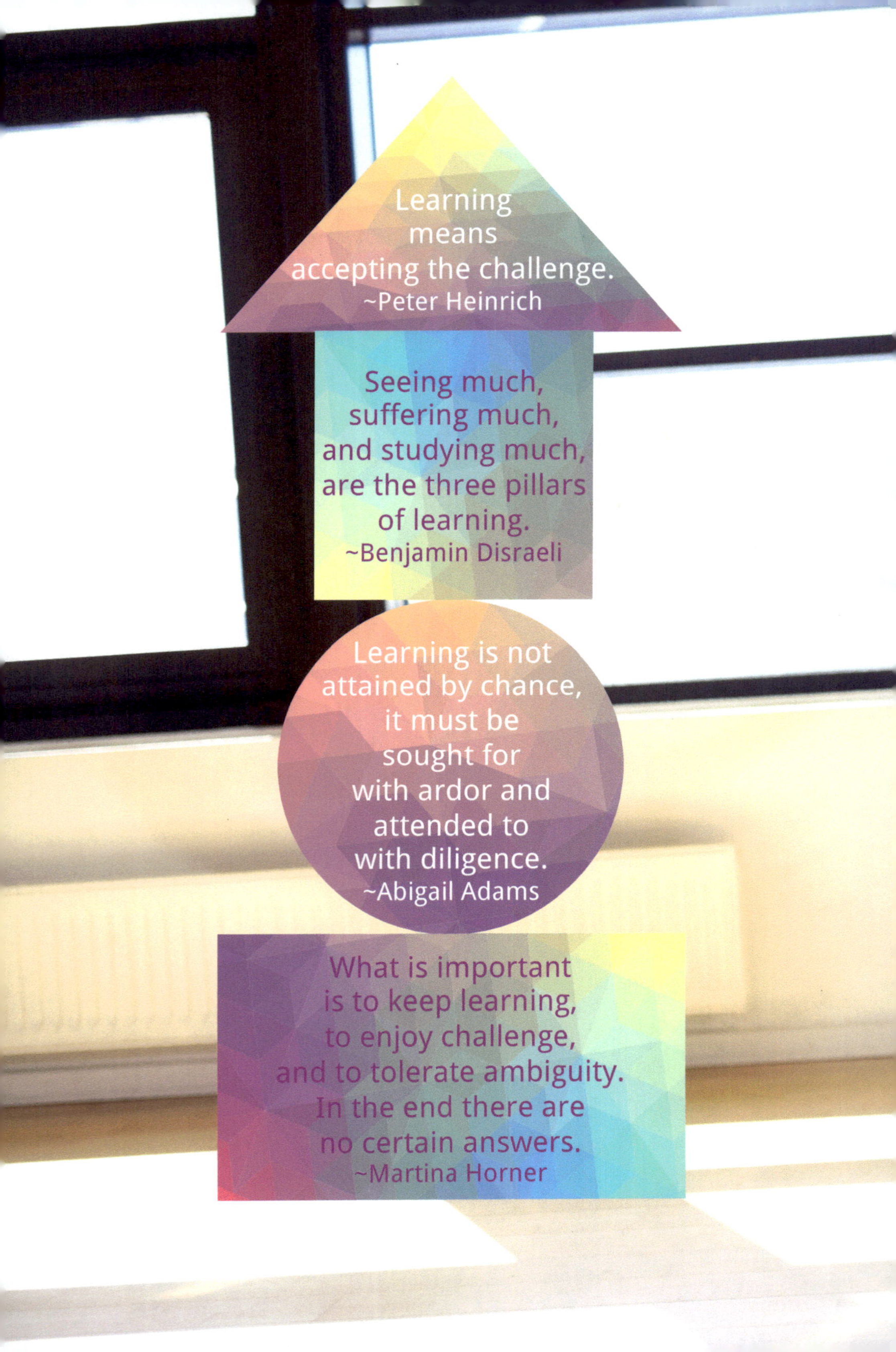

Learning
means
accepting the challenge.
~Peter Heinrich

Seeing much,
suffering much,
and studying much,
are the three pillars
of learning.
~Benjamin Disraeli

Learning is not
attained by chance,
it must be
sought for
with ardor and
attended to
with diligence.
~Abigail Adams

What is important
is to keep learning,
to enjoy challenge,
and to tolerate ambiguity.
In the end there are
no certain answers.
~Martina Horner

Challenge
A happy life is
one, spent
in learning,
earning,
and yearning.
~Lillian Gish

All Senses

There are
so many things
you can learn about,
but you'll miss
the best things
if you keep
your eyes shut.
~Theodor Seuss Geisel

I have
always gotten
a thrill, a kick, from
learning new things.
~Cynthia Kenyon

I used to be really
insecure about my
self-education.
I'm definitely
always learning. But
there's many ways to learn.
There are many, many ways
to always be a learner.
~Maggie Grace

Learning to draw
is really a matter of
learning to see –
to see correctly –
and that means a good
deal more than merely
looking with the eye.
~Kimon Nicolaides

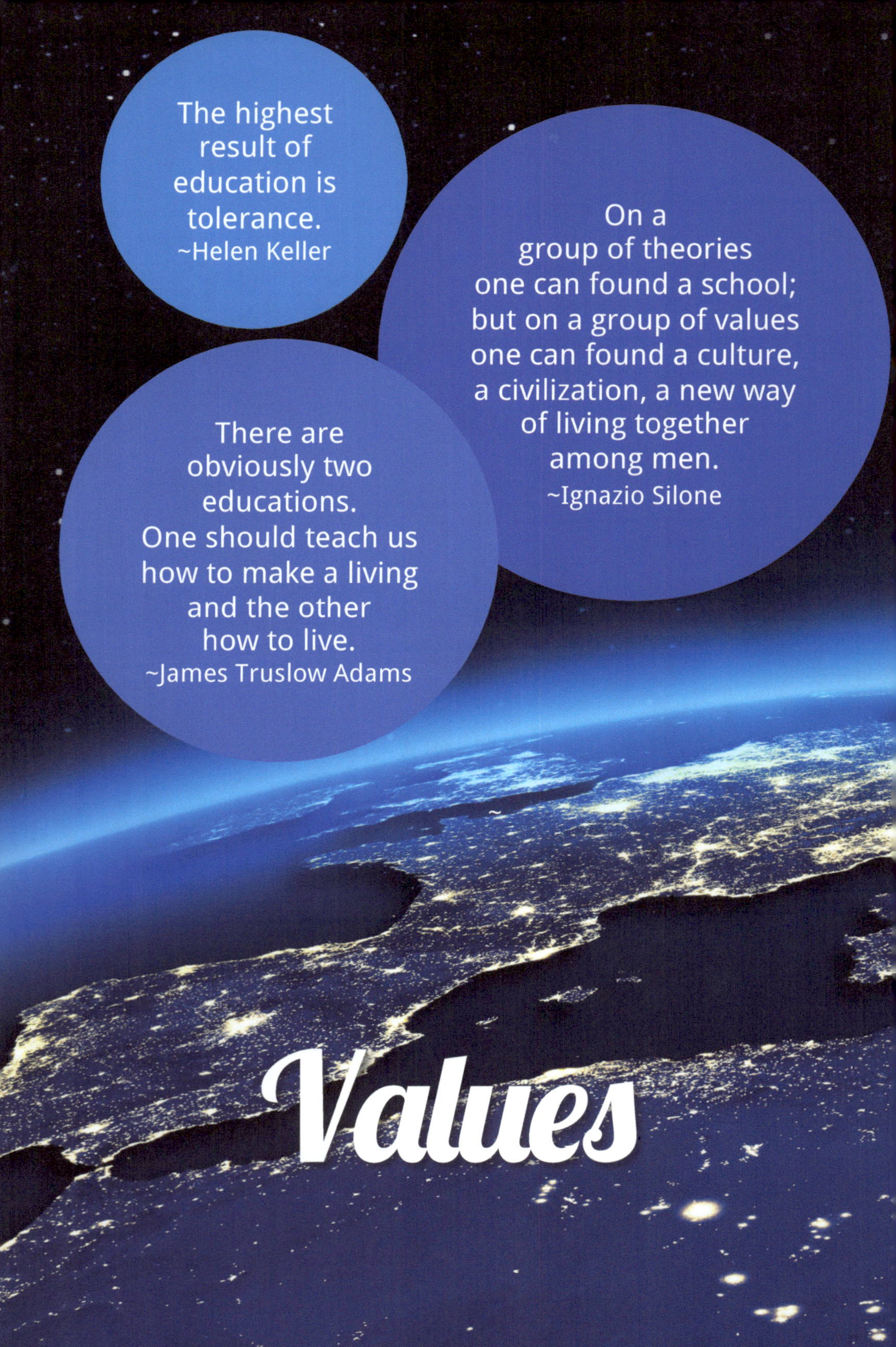
The highest result of education is tolerance.
~Helen Keller

On a group of theories one can found a school; but on a group of values one can found a culture, a civilization, a new way of living together among men.
~Ignazio Silone

There are obviously two educations. One should teach us how to make a living and the other how to live.
~James Truslow Adams

Values

The aim of education is the knowledge not of fact, but of
VALUES
WILLIAM RALPH INGE

Education

The direction in which education starts a man will determine his future life.
~Plato

EDUCATION IS LIFE ITSELF.
JOHN DEWEY

Education is like a double-edged sword. It may be turned to dangerous uses if it is not properly handled.
~Wu Ting-Fang

Natural ability without education has more often attained to glory and virtue than natural without education without natural ability.
~Cicero
Education is the best provision for old age.
~Aristotle
Genius without education is like silver in the mine.
~Benjamin Franklin

Leadership

Leadership and learning are indispensable to each other.
~John F. Kennedy

Innovation distinguishes between a leader and a follower.
~Steve Jobs

By learning to obey, you will know how to command.
~Italian Proverb

If you think
education is expensive,
try ignorance!
~Andy McIntyre

Let ignorance
talk as it will,
learning
has its value.
~Jean de La Fontaine

KNOWLEDGE

IGNORANCE

The learning
and knowledge
that we have, is,
at the most,
but little
compared
with that of which
we are ignorant.
~Plato

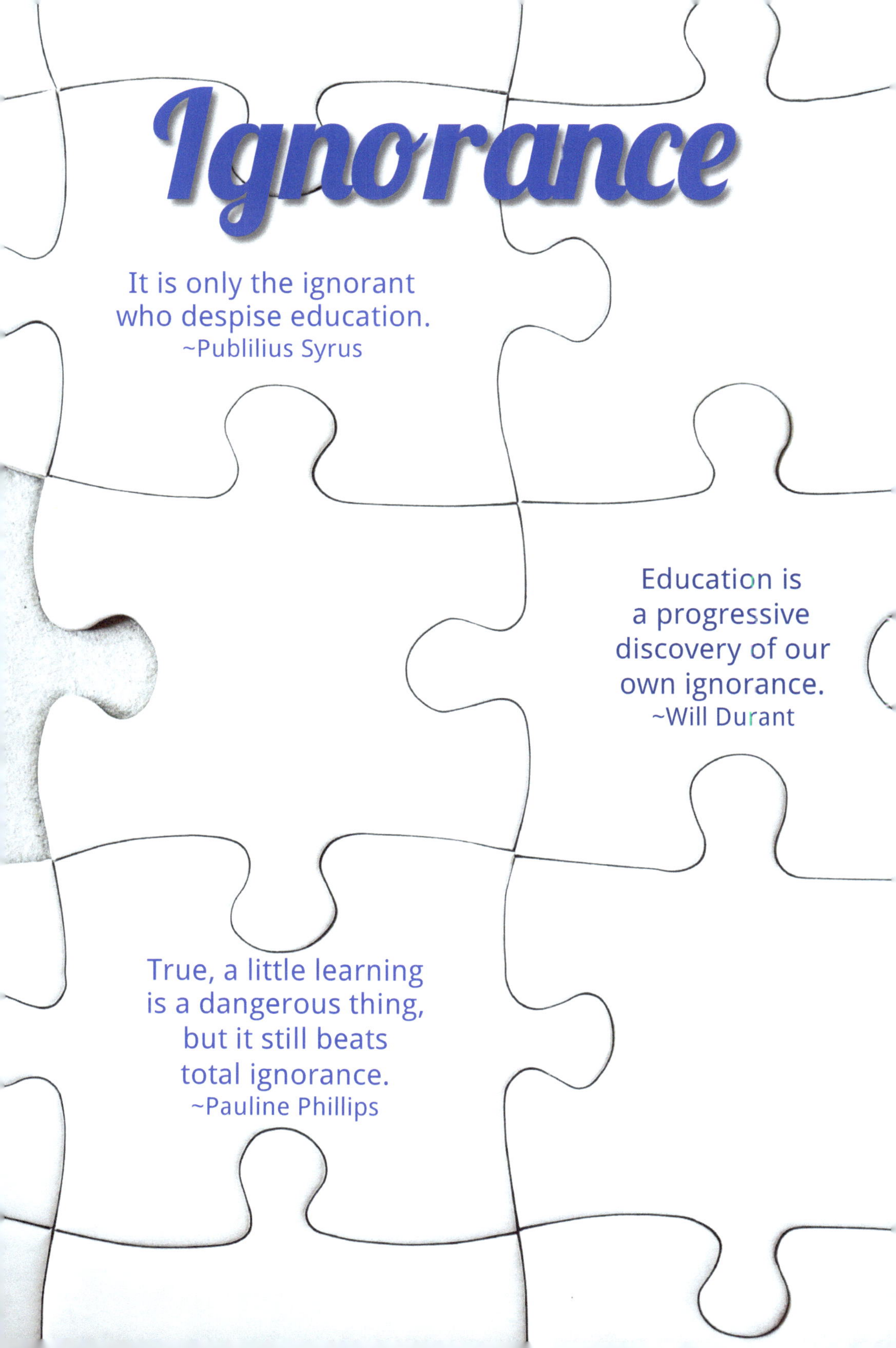

Ignorance

It is only the ignorant
who despise education.
~Publilius Syrus

Education is
a progressive
discovery of our
own ignorance.
~Will Durant

True, a little learning
is a dangerous thing,
but it still beats
total ignorance.
~Pauline Phillips

Setbacks

Setbacks are just
learning experiences.
~Beth Brooke

When you win a lot,
you don't learn much.
with my ups and downs,
it's a lot of learning.
~Tina Maze

What is defeat?
Nothing but education;
nothing but the first step
to something better.
~Wendell Phillips

There are no secrets to success.
It is the result of preparation,
hard work, and
learning from failure.
~Colin Powell

We should regret our mistakes
and learn from them,
but never carry them forward
into the future with us.
~Lucy Maud Montgomery

Treasure

Poverty must not be
a bar to learning and learning
must offer an escape
from poverty.
~Lyndon B. Johnson

The beautiful thing about
learning is nobody can
take it away from you.
~B. B. King

Learning
makes a man
fit company for
himself.
~Thomas Fuller

SUCCESS
Learning is
a treasure that will
FOLLOW
its owner everywhere.
CHINESE PROVERB

You aren't learning anything when you're TALKING
LYNDON B. JOHNSON

Declutter

Learning to ignore things
is one of the great paths
to inner peace.
~Robert J. Sawyer

The process of learning
requires not only hearing
and applying but also
forgetting and then
remembering again.
~John Gray

More important
than learning how to recall things
is finding ways to forget things
that are cluttering the mind.
~James Waddell Alexander

Wisdom

Wisdom is not a
product of schooling,
but of the life-long
attempt to
acquire it.
~Albert Einstein

You can buy
education,
but wisdom is
a gift from God.
~Author Unknown

A wise system
of education
will at last teach us
how little man
yet knows,
how much he has
still to learn.
~John Lubbock

Wisdom is
learning
what
to overlook.
~William James

I am still learning.
MICHELANGELO

Lifelong Learning

Live as if your were to die tomorrow. Learn as if you were to live forever.
~Mahatma Gandhi

The education of a man is never completed until he dies.
~Robert E. Lee

Learning is what most adults will do for a living in the 21st century.
~Alfred Edward Perlman

We now accept the fact that learning is a lifelong process of keeping abreast of change. And the most pressing task is to teach people how to learn.
~Peter Drucker

My Favorite Quotes About Learning

My Favorite Quotes About Learning

FREE BONUS

As a thank you for buying this "learning book",
I'm offering all readers my ebook
"Inspirational Picture Quotes about Friendship" for **FREE.**

According to new research, true happiness lies in rewarding relationships,
not material wealth. Even if we as individuals can understand
the importance of close relationships on a social level,
some of us often forget that such relationships
are actually necessary for our own personal happiness.

You can download
"Inspirational Picture Quotes about Friendship" for FREE
by following the link below:

=> **http://leanjumpstart.com/friendship9cs**

OTHER BOOKS BY GABI RUPP IN THIS SERIES

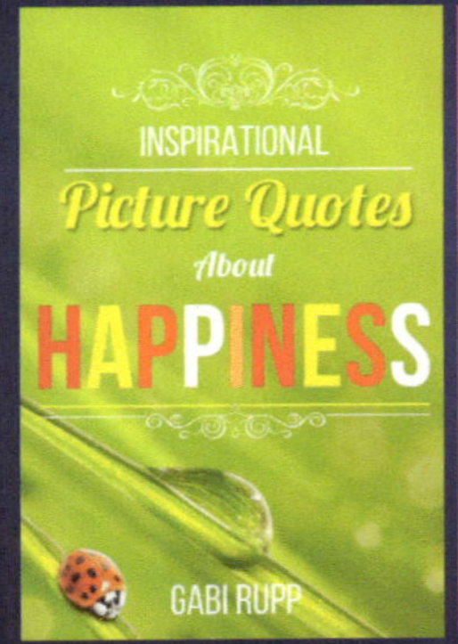

Gabi Rupp is a certified coach, author and entrepreneur. Prior to her work online, Gabi spent more than a decade as a marketing executive, mostly in the food and nutrition field, helping her clients realize their own projects. After her daughter was born, she found her true calling: writing, teaching, and coaching. Having the perfect life/work balance gave her the freedom to be a fulltime mother. In 2013 she founded leanjumpstart.com, where she uses a successful combination of proven science and practical experience to help people get in shape and stick with their new, healthy habits. Gabi is now happily settled in a little German town near the beautiful Black Forest region and spends her days with family, friends, and assisting clients as they overcome limitations and live life to its fullest potential.

Publisher: Gabi Rupp, Leanjumpstart.com /
gabi@leanjumpstart.com
Concept, Design & Layout: Gabi Rupp
Photo Credits: Footage Firm Inc., Dollar Photo Club ©:
Андрей Козаченко, connel_design, Lokisurina,
milicanistoran, mudretsov, Myst
Gabi Rupp, stanciuc, UBER IMAGES, Alan Z. Uster
ISBN-13: 978-1517036331
ISBN-10: 151703633X